Touching Tomorrow

A play

Gillian Plowman

Samuel French—London
New York-Toronto-Hollywood

FOR AMATEUR PRODUCTION ENQUIRIES

UNITED KINGDOM AND WORLD
EXCLUDING NORTH AMERICA
plays@samuelfrench.co.uk
020 7255 4302/01

Each title is subject to availability from Samuel French,
depending upon country of performance.

CHARACTERS

Vincent, learning disabilities; 50s
Dorcas, his sister, who lives with and cares for him; 50s
Gemma, a homeless lodger; 25
Kate, a friend of Dorcas, local reporter; any age
Sholto, a friend of Vincent, lives with his parents; any age

SYNOPSIS OF SCENES

The action takes place in the house of Dorcas and Vincent

SCENE 1 Tuesday
SCENE 2 A little later on the same day
SCENE 3 Later that evening
SCENE 4 The next day. One o' clock
SCENE 5 Later the same day
SCENE 6 The next morning

Time—the present

MUSIC

A licence issued by Samuel French Ltd to perform this play does not include permission to use the Incidental music specified in this copy. Where the place of performance is already licensed by the PERFORMING RIGHT SOCIETY a return of the music used must be made to them. If the place of performance is not so licensed then application should be made to the PERFORMING RIGHT SOCIETY, 29 Berners Street, London W1.

A separate and additional licence from PHONOGRAPHIC PERFORMANCES LTD, 1 Upper James Street, London W1R 3HG is needed whenever commercial recordings are used.

TOUCHING TOMORROW

Scene 1

Dorcas's and Vincent's house. Tuesday

The house is bright and nice and lived-in with a selection of easy chairs, none matching but all interesting. There is a door to the kitchen and a door to the hall

Dorcas brings in Gemma. Dorcas is in her fifties and is the administrator for the local council "bulky waste" department. She wears a blouse and skirt but with a cardigan rather than jacket. She carries some plastic bags containing clothes from Oxfam. Gemma is twenty-five and homeless. She is roughly dressed and carries a pile of unsold copies of the Big Issue

Dorcas Come in.
Gemma Thanks.
Dorcas Vincent isn't home yet.
Gemma Are you sure he won't mind?
Dorcas No. Don't worry. No. He'll love you to death.

Beat

    Sorry ... Bad choice of words ... I mean he takes to people. He'll take to you.
Gemma I ...
Dorcas It's all right. Really. Put the papers through there under the kitchen table.
Gemma I didn't sell many today.
Dorcas You were traumatized. I could see that.

Gemma Could you?

Dorcas Yes.

Gemma How?

Dorcas By looking at you.

Gemma People don't look at you when they buy the *Big Issue*.

Dorcas Well at least they're buying one. Presumably that's all you want from most people.

Gemma You always look at me.

Dorcas Well …

Gemma You do, yes. And you smile.

Dorcas And you usually smile back. But not today.

Gemma No.

Dorcas I knew something was wrong. I've known you for quite a while.

Gemma Buying a paper once a week amounts to knowing someone, does it?

Dorcas Today you looked terrible.

Gemma Traumatized you said.

Dorcas Yes.

Pause. Gemma stands still

I wondered where you slept.

Gemma You never asked.

Dorcas It seemed nosy somehow. Not my business.

Gemma In a tent by the canal.

Dorcas Yes.

Gemma If you'd asked before, what would you have done?

Dorcas I work for the council. Not in the right department. I'm in rubbish. But I could have talked to someone …

Gemma sways

Sit down.

Gemma In these things?

Dorcas Sit down before you fall down.

Gemma Where?

Dorcas Anywhere!
Gemma Which is your chair?
Dorcas It doesn't matter.
Gemma I'd rather know.
Dorcas I usually sit here and Vincent likes that chair. He hangs his legs over the side.
Gemma (*indicating a third chair*) Shall I sit here then?
Dorcas That's fine.
Gemma You've got to know where it's all right to be. (*She sits in the chair*)
Dorcas And they would have talked to social services. You're a vulnerable young woman. You shouldn't be sleeping rough.
Gemma But you didn't ask.

Beat

Dorcas I'll come to the police with you.
Gemma No. They'll look at me and say, "It's you again. What have you been up to this time?" And they won't believe me. And they'll look at you and say, "Don't be stupid, Mrs ——"
Dorcas Not married.
Gemma "Taking her in. She'll bring you nothing but trouble."
Dorcas No they won't.
Gemma That's what they'll say. In fact they probably won't let you.
Dorcas What?
Gemma Take me in.
Dorcas They'll be pleased you've got somewhere safe to go.
Gemma They won't care about my safety, they'll care about yours.
Dorcas I'm in no danger.
Gemma They'll tell you you are.
Dorcas They can't stop me.
Gemma They'll poison you against me.
Dorcas Why would they do that?

Pause

Gemma?

Gemma Because they gave me a room in a hostel and I couldn't live
    in it.
Dorcas Why not?
Gemma The noise. And the people. I couldn't keep them out …
Dorcas What people?
Gemma Other people at the hostel. The door wouldn't close and
    they kept coming in and they raped me.
Dorcas In the hostel?
Gemma Yes.
Dorcas *They* did?
Gemma They. He.
Dorcas He who?
Gemma In the hostel.

Beat

Dorcas Did you tell anyone?
Gemma No.
Dorcas Why not?
Gemma Because I knew him.

Beat

Dorcas And in your tent last night?
Gemma Yes.
Dorcas You were raped?
Gemma Yes.
Dorcas You've been raped twice?
Gemma Yes.
Dorcas Was it the same person?
Gemma No.
Dorcas You *must* tell the police.
Gemma No.
Dorcas You must.
Gemma Have you ever been raped?
Dorcas No.
Gemma You don't go to the police.

Dorcas Then you must see a doctor. You could be hurt.
Gemma I knew them. (*She begins to shake*)
Dorcas I'll make a cup of tea.
Gemma No-one believes you if you know them.

Tiny beat

Dorcas I believe you.
Gemma When you sleep rough, it's like there's nothing between
  you and evil. No bricks, no doors, no locks. You can't keep it out.
Dorcas Not everybody's evil.

Gemma looks at her

Gemma Do you lock your doors at night?
Dorcas Well, yes.

Silence

  I thought there was a sort of camaraderie.

Gemma looks at her some more

  On the streets. People looking out for each other. I'm wrong.
Gemma Yes, you're fucking wrong.
Dorcas Sorry.
Gemma Sorry.
Dorcas *I understand.*
Gemma What?
Dorcas Nothing.
Gemma Nothing.
Dorcas I don't know anything about it.
Gemma I don't mean to be like this.
Dorcas I know you don't.
Gemma You're right. Sometimes it's OK. Down the canal, there's
  a few of us. Share a fire. Food. Then it goes wrong. There's
  nothing that says where the line is and you get invaded.

Dorcas You won't get invaded here.
Gemma I'll try to …
Dorcas I'll try and help.
Gemma Living like I have ...
Dorcas I know.
Gemma I can't believe that you've done this.

Dorcas gives her a tiny hug

Dorcas Nor can I!
Gemma There's no crosses anywhere.
Dorcas It's not a religious thing.
Gemma Menopausal thing?

Dorcas laughs

Dorcas More likely. Why don't you have a soak in the bath and I'll bring the tea up? Then you can take your pick from Oxfam's latest designs or have a look through my wardrobe and see what'll fit you.

Dorcas gives Gemma the plastic bags

Gemma Anything?
Dorcas What?
Gemma From your wardrobe?
Dorcas Mmm.
Gemma Nobody likes other people to wear their clothes.
Dorcas I don't mind. I'm not a fashion plate. Clothes are clothes. Which probably means that you'll find my things very dull. But clean.
Gemma Of course.

Tiny beat

Dorcas Whereas you chose all this stuff, so mix and match!

Pause

You should go to the police.
Gemma No.
Dorcas Rape's a terrible thing.
Gemma Not when you're used to it.
Dorcas You can't — you can't ... it's not something you get used to.
Gemma What would you rather do? Sit in a poxy police station, being interrogated for hours by coppers and social workers, being raped all over again by doctors with instruments collecting evidence, knowing they don't believe you. Knowing that the person who raped you will turn round and say she was up for it. She's up for it every night. Why was last night any different? *Because last night I didn't want to! I don't want to! I never want to! Nobody understands! (She breaks down)*
Dorcas It's all right.

Gemma sobs and holds on to Dorcas

I understand.
Gemma Or would you rather be in a hot bath with somebody nice bringing you tea and clean clothes and a bed of your own in a room with a door.
Dorcas The door doesn't lock but it stays shut.
Gemma What would you rather?

Dorcas nods

Dorcas Come on then. Let's find your room and run your bath.

There is a banging on the front door and the sound of a key in the lock

Vincent. Do you want to meet him before or after?
Gemma After.

Dorcas leads Gemma quickly out to the hall and they disappear as Vincent enters the room

Vincent, in his fifties, is Dorcas's brother and has learning difficulties. He is in a happy mood, having been to the day centre, and made and learnt to work a yo-yo. He drops his bag and his coat where he stands and proceeds to play with the yo-yo. He loves Beatles songs and sings "Lucy in the Sky with Diamonds"

Dorcas returns

Vincent Look, Dorcas!
Dorcas What's that?
Vincent A yo-yo! It's mine. I made it. This is how you do it!
Dorcas Very good!
Vincent I'm skilful.
Dorcas Who told you that?
Vincent Brian.
Dorcas Well, he ought to know.
Vincent Yes.
Dorcas (*inspecting the yo-yo*) Did you make the yo-yo yourself?
Vincent Yes!
Dorcas Well done. That's wonderful. Did everyone make one?
Vincent Sholto did.
Dorcas Is his yellow?
Vincent No. His is red. See if you can do it.
Dorcas I don't think I'm as skilful as you.
Vincent No.

Dorcas tries to make the yo-yo work but is (deliberately) no good at it. Vincent is full of glee

Dorcas I can't do it.
Vincent No.
Dorcas Can you show me how to do it.

Vincent makes the yo-yo work

Tell me how you do it.

Vincent Like that. (*He shows her*)
Dorcas Like what?
Vincent That! Up and down.
Dorcas Tell me how you make it go up and down like that, Vincent.
Vincent No!

Beat

Dorcas Can I practise with it later?
Vincent You can. I'll put it there. (*He places it carefully*)
Dorcas Vincent, we've got a guest.
Vincent Yes.
Dorcas A nice young lady called Gemma.
Vincent That's a dog's name.
Dorcas Yes, Gemma down the road.
Vincent Here. Gemma. Gemma, Gemma … (*He whistles*)
Dorcas It's a lady's name and Gemma's a lady dog and our guest
 is a lady too.
Vincent Where is Gemma?
Dorcas She's having a bath at the moment.
Vincent Is it her bedtime?
Dorcas I think she's very tired and might well go to bed early. But
 we'll have supper first. I know you'll be kind to her, Vincent —
 she's had a hard time.
Vincent Yes. (*He sings "A Hard Day's Night"*)
Dorcas (*over this*) I'm going to take a cup of tea up to her in the bath.
 Would you like one?
Vincent In the bath?
Dorcas No, here.
Vincent Sholto's coming round for a beer.
Dorcas Is he? You didn't ask me.
Vincent You didn't ask me.

Beat

Dorcas What?
Vincent If Gemma could come round.

Dorcas is surprised at his logic

Dorcas So do we have any beer?

Vincent doesn't know

Vincent He's bringing his yo-yo.
Dorcas Is he coming for supper?

Vincent knows

Vincent After supper.
Dorcas So have a cup of tea now, eh?
Vincent Mmm.
Dorcas Pick those things up and put them away.

Dorcas goes out to the kitchen

The phone rings and Vincent answers it

Vincent (*into the phone*) Hallo, Kate. ... Yes, Kate. ... I did, Kate.

Dorcas enters and listens

I made a yo-yo, Kate. ... She's here, Kate. ... I will, Kate. ...
Goodbye, Kate. (*He holds the receiver out to Dorcas*) It's Kate.
Dorcas (*into the phone*) Hallo, Kate. Thank goodness you're not
called Hermione! ...

Dorcas looks at Vincent who starts to sing "Hello Goodbye"

I'd love to see it, but I've got someone staying. ... You can go to
the cinema on your own! ... The girl who sells *Big Issue*s on the
corner of West Street. ... Because I felt sorry for her. ... Because
— she's living rough and ... She was attacked. (*To Vincent*)
Shush, Vincent. (*Into the phone*) Stop being a reporter. ... I don't
know. ... I don't know. ... I don't know. ... (*To Vincent*) *Shush!*
Vincent Who is it?
Dorcas It's Hermione.

Vincent is puzzled

Vincent No it's not.
Dorcas (*into the phone*) No, I don't. ... No, you can't. ... Go to the
  cinema, Kate, and write a pungent review!
Vincent It's Kate.
Dorcas *After* supper then. (*She puts the phone down*)

Vincent sings some of the chorus of "She Loves You"

Black-out

SCENE 2

The same. A little later on the same day

*Vincent is sitting in his chair listening to a Beatles tape, his body
moving in time to the music. He holds his yo-yo and drinks a mug
of tea*

Gemma enters, clean and refreshed, carrying her empty mug

Gemma Hallo.
Vincent (*jumping to his feet and spilling tea down his t-shirt*) Hallo.
  Oh ...(*He tries to wipe himself down, drops the mug, drops the yo-
  yo and looks at her speechlessly*)
Gemma Are you all right?

He nods. She picks up his mug and looks for Dorcas

  I'm Gemma.

*Vincent whistles as though at the dog Gemma. They both stand, not
knowing what to say*

  Dorcas enters and turns the music down

Dorcas Gemma, you look lovely. Vincent, this is Gemma. Vincent, you don't look lovely. What have you done? Gemma, this is my brother, Vincent.
Gemma He spilt his tea.
Vincent It doesn't matter.
Dorcas No, of course it doesn't. Accidents will happen. Go and put a clean t-shirt on.

Vincent goes

Vincent has learning difficulties.
Gemma How old is he?
Dorcas Ask him. Do you like pasta?
Gemma Yes. Why won't you tell me?
Dorcas Because the answer is one of his favourite sayings.
Gemma In the olden days, he would have been the village idiot, wouldn't he?

Beat

Dorcas With tuna and sweetcorn?
Gemma Sounds wonderful. Can I help?
Dorcas You can help Vincent wash up afterwards.

Beat

Dunce, they called him when he was at school. It's all so different now. I wish he was starting out again.
Gemma Like me.

She sits in Dorcas's special chair and yawns. Dorcas looks at her

Are you sure I can't do anything?

Beat

Dorcas You just relax.

Gemma It's the hot bath. And everything.
Dorcas I know. You can go to bed as soon as you've had supper if
    you like. I'm sure you'll sleep soundly.
Gemma Bed. It's such a beautiful bed. Bed. Such a beautiful sound.
    The sound of bed. The bed of sounds. Sound sleep. You are my
    saviour.
Dorcas No …
Gemma I don't want to be a worry to you.
Dorcas There's nothing to worry about.
Gemma Except the washing-up.

Beat

Dorcas Well, there's always tomorrow. You can do it then.

Vincent returns with a clean shirt

Vincent Gemma, do you want to see if you can do my yo-yo?

*Dorcas tries to indicate to Gemma that she shouldn't be able to do
it but Gemma ignores her. Vincent hands the yo-yo to Gemma who
manages it very well. Vincent hides his disappointment*

    That's very skilful.
Gemma Not really. It's easy.

Silence

Black-out

SCENE 3

The same. Later that evening

*The meal is finished and Vincent clears the table, coming and going
out to the kitchen with two items at a time. It is his job. From the
kitchen comes the sound of the Beatles. Vincent sings along. Dorcas
is sitting at the table*

Dorcas There's more things with three people eating, Vincent. Shall I help?
Vincent No. It's my job.

The doorbell rings

Dorcas Sholto or Kate?
Vincent Sholto!

Dorcas goes to answer the front door

Vincent (*rushing to do his chores*) Sholto. Sholto. Sholto.

Dorcas enters with Kate

Sholto. Sholto. Sholto.
Dorcas Kate.
Kate Hallo, Vincent.
Vincent Sholto's coming.
Kate Am I a disappointment?
Vincent Yes.
Kate Where's your guest?
Dorcas Gone to bed.

Kate looks at her watch

She can't remember when she last slept in a bed.

Kate gets out a notebook and pen and plonks herself at the table

Stop it, Hermione. This isn't a story.
Vincent (*at the table*) That's Kate.

Vincent goes to the kitchen

Kate Listen, Miss Bulky Waste, there you are, working for the council organizing the removal of large items of rubbish from people's lives, an ordinary woman who lives a quiet life with her bachelor brother ...

The music suddenly gets turned up in the kitchen

Vincent comes back

Dorcas Turn it down, Vincent! (*To Kate*) Not so quiet.
Vincent I can't hear it when I'm in here. (*He goes to turn on the sitting-room music*)
Dorcas This one in here's for when you're in here and that one out there's for when you're out there. (*To Kate*) We have this every night. (*To Vincent*) No, don't turn this one on in here. We're talking. It's taking all night to clear the table, Vincent. Go and start the washing up. I'll clear the rest.

Vincent goes out to the kitchen

Turn it down!

The music volume is reduced from the kitchen

This quiet life? (*She puts the rest of the things neatly on a tray*)
Kate All right. A hard-working woman with two full-time jobs.
Dorcas Two?
Kate Bulky waste and Vincent. Then you suddenly go and scoop up a homeless person. Why?
Dorcas Shut up.
Kate There's an interested reading public.
Dorcas Spare bedrooms.

Dorcas takes the tray to the kitchen

Kate Is it for just tonight or is she staying?

Dorcas enters and sits at the table with Kate

Dorcas Till she finds somewhere of her own.
Kate Why hasn't she got somewhere of her own?
Dorcas I don't know.

Kate Didn't you ask?

Dorcas Not yet.

Kate An intriguing story.

Dorcas It isn't a story.

Kate Oh yes it is. "Woman takes homeless stranger into already difficult family situation. What happens next? Will it work? Will she regret it? Will they fall out. Will she never be able to get rid of homeless stranger?" Our readers will be avid followers of the plot.

Dorcas It's not a difficult family situation. I'm living with my bachelor brother.

Kate You've devoted yourself to Vincent. Sacrificed your life for him.

Dorcas No I haven't! We live together in our parents' home, that's all.

Kate You have to look after him.

Dorcas No I don't.

Kate Now you're looking after a complete stranger. How's that going to work out?

Dorcas I don't know!

There is a crashing from the kitchen

Dorcas (*looking at Kate*) It's all plastic. (*She grins*)
Kate What made you do it, Dorcas?

Vincent enters and gives Dorcas two halves of a broken plastic plate

Good job you hadn't washed it up first, Vincent. That would have been a waste.

Vincent laughs and goes out to the kitchen

Lunchtime I went out. Got a baguette. Bar of chocolate. Shouldn't have. Bought my *Big Issue* and thought, I'll give her my lunch. Do without. Do me good. I started to say, "Would you ..." And she looked at me like — she needed me. Like I was her saviour.

Kate They're good at that.

Beat

Sorry. Go on.
Dorcas I thought, if I don't take her home, she'll die.
Kate Oh, come on.
Dorcas No, it was that strong. If I don't take her home, she'll die. Not this minute, not today. But she's given up on herself. She'll die.
Kate This doesn't sound like Miss Practical Efficient Bulky Waste.
Dorcas They live in a tent down by the canal, you see and one of them raped her.
Kate She told you.

Dorcas nods

Kate She should have told the police.
Dorcas That's a trauma in itself.
Kate Why you?
Dorcas Why me? Indeed why me? For a reason.
Kate What made her tell you?
Dorcas Because I said, "what's happened to you …?"
Kate I'm a cynic.
Dorcas Why?
Kate I think she saw you coming.
Dorcas She was raped by one of a group of people she has no option but to sleep with. She's a rape victim with no credence and she didn't want to put herself through an interrogation.
Kate Strong stuff. (*She makes notes*)
Dorcas Write about it then. Let people round here know that homelessness and all its horrors happens right on our doorstep. And somebody has to do something. She's a really nice person, Kate.
Kate What's her name?
Dorcas Gemma. Call it Gemma's story.
Kate Oh no, Dorcas. It's your story.

The doorbell rings

Vincent rushes in from the kitchen

Vincent Sholto. Sholto. Sholto.

Vincent rushes across the room and goes out to the front door

Dorcas Sholto's come for a beer. I'm taking them both to the tip
   tomorrow. They've got a day's shovelling.
Kate Dorcas, you're a star, do you know that?
Dorcas Write about Gemma.

Vincent leads Sholto in

*Sholto is very excitable and kisses Dorcas and Kate soundly. He
gives Dorcas a carrier bag containing a large plastic bottle of beer*

Sholto Smackeroo, Dorcs. Smackeroo, Katie.
Kate How come he shortens yours and lengthens mine?
Sholto Smackeroo, Vinny!
Vincent Smackeroo, Sholto!

*They dance around singing to the music. Dorcas takes the beer out
of the bag and gets four glasses*

Sholto My mum says will you ring her to say I didn't open it on the
   way.
Dorcas I will.

*Vincent and Sholto get the yo-yos and make them work, still singing.
Dorcas makes the phone call. Kate claps loudly*

Kate Well done, that's very clever.
Vincent Skilful.
Dorcas Would you like to pour the beer, Vincent? Carefully.

*Vincent pours the beer without spilling any but the glasses are too
full to lift so they all have to bend down to sup*

   (*Into the phone*) Hallo, it's Dorcas. Mission accomplished.

Sholto My mum said only to have one beer because tomorrow's a
   working day and we have to be fit.

Dorcas bends down to sup her beer

Vincent Not drunk.
Sholto Or we'll get the sack.
Dorcas Definitely only one beer so make it last.
Sholto I've got some new overalls, because I put holes in the other
   ones and my mum said they were old anyway and I was working
   very hard so that's how it happened.
Vincent Are you going to wear them tomorrow?
Sholto Yes.

Vincent looks at Dorcas

Dorcas You haven't got holes in yours.
Kate Bet he will by the end of tomorrow.

Now they can pick up the glasses

Vincent Cheers!
Sholto Cheers!
Dorcas Cheers!
Kate Cheers!

*Vincent puts on his sitting-room music so that two lots of music are
heard now*

Dorcas Vincent, go and turn the other one off!

Vincent goes to the kitchen, turns off the music and returns

Sholto is singing along and working his yo-yo

Sholto Made it myself!
Kate Brilliant!

Gemma comes storming in

Gemma What are you doing? I can't sleep! I can't fucking get to sleep!

The music plays through the silence. Dorcas switches it off in the sitting-room and then goes to put her arm round Gemma

Dorcas We've been very noisy. Sholto's going home now, aren't you?
Vincent He hasn't finished his beer.

Sholto picks up his glass and downs the beer. He burps and smiles happily

Sholto Goodbye, Vinny.
Vincent Goodbye, Sholto.
Sholto Goodbye, Katie.
Kate Goodbye, Sholto, see you again soon.
Sholto Goodbye, Dorcs.
Dorcas I'll pick you up in the morning at half-past eight.
Sholto Goodbye …?
Dorcas Gemma.
Sholto (*turning to Vincent excitedly*) Gemma, the dog!

Vincent whistles

Sholto
Vincent } (*together*) Here, Gemma, Gemma, Gemma!
Dorcas Vincent! See Sholto out.

Vincent and Sholto bounce their way out noisily

Gemma, Kate's a friend of mine and she writes for the local paper. Maybe it would help if she wrote about you, what you've been through.

Gemma Help who?

Dorcas You. Other women in your circumstances. Why you're homeless. Why you feel you can't go to the police. The terrible things that happen that — someone ought to do something about ——

Gemma You're doing something about it.

Dorcas Kate can do more. Can't you, Kate?

Kate A personal story always pricks people's consciences.

Gemma I just want to go to sleep.

Kate Think about it. We could change your name or it could be anonymous. I'll call round tomorrow …

Vincent enters singing "A Hard Day's Night"

Dorcas When Vincent's at work.

Gemma Shut up!

Vincent shuts up

Dorcas Gemma's very tired and she needs us all to be quiet so that she can go to sleep.

Vincent understands and tiptoes to his chair and sits, staying quiet

Kate Shall I read this week's story?

Vincent nods, being quiet. Kate gets the local paper out of her bag

(*Reading*) "'The Goose Nanny' by Kate Pritchard."

Vincent points to her, still being quiet

That's me.

The conversation between Gemma and Dorcas overlaps Kate's reading

Gemma I really didn't mean to ——

Dorcas You need a good night's sleep.

Gemma You wish you hadn't done it now, don't you?

Dorcas You'll feel better tomorrow.

Gemma Don't you?

Dorcas Of course not.

Gemma You want me to leave.

Dorcas No I don't.

Kate (*reading*) "Once again, on the Hardwick canal, Gertie the Goose has taken over responsibility for eight new cygnets hatched on Wednesday. Every year, a pair of swans return to breed on the canal, and for the past three years, Gertie has been there to take charge. She watches over the cygnets, often whilst both swans take a nap, leads them in single file as they take their daily swim, and generally warns off any possible foes ..."

Vincent What are foes?
Kate Enemies.
Vincent On the canal?
Gemma Yes. Enemies on the canal. You have to beware them.

Gemma turns and goes out up to bed

Black-out

Scene 4

The same. One o'clock the next day

There is bright sunshine

Gemma enters from the kitchen. She's wearing a dressing-gown and carries a mug of coffee

The doorbell rings

She goes out to answer it and enters, followed by Kate

Kate Five past one. Halfway through the day.
Gemma So?
Kate Have you just got up?
Gemma Yes.
Kate You slept well in the end then?
Gemma Yes.
Kate Have you just made that?
Gemma Yes.

Beat

Kate I'll get myself one.

Kate puts her bag down and goes out to the kitchen

Gemma looks at her bag and then goes to look in it

Kate enters with a mug of coffee and sees her

Gemma?
Gemma Have you got any fags?
Kate Don't smoke.
Gemma You should have some though.
Kate To offer to people like you?
Gemma If you want to interview them.
Kate You're happy to be interviewed?
Gemma Don't know.

Kate gets a new packet of cigarettes from her jacket pocket and gives it to Gemma

Kate I bought them on the way here.

Gemma takes a cigarette out

Dorcas won't like it.
Gemma Won't she?

Kate No-one smokes in her house.

Gemma Has she forbidden it?

Kate I don't think so. People know she doesn't like it and they
respect that.

Gemma You obviously don't.

Kate It's a question of priorities.

Gemma goes out to the kitchen

Kate finds her notebook and pen

Gemma comes back with a box of matches

Where are you from?

Gemma All over. Army father. Bully. Dead mother. (*She lights the
cigarette*)

Kate When did she die?

Gemma Eight years ago. I killed her.

Silence

I was seventeen. Just passed my driving test. My father was
drinking in the mess and rang me to pick him up. She was leaving
the house to do her nightshift at the hospital. He was singing at the
top of his voice and lurching about. Impeding me, they said. I hit
her. She went to the hospital and died of her injuries. He was
dismissed from the army, they took the married quarters back and
I was fucked.

Kate Where did he go?

Gemma Overseas. He liked it overseas. Don't ask me where. I
wouldn't have gone with him if you paid me.

Kate makes notes

Dramatic enough for you?

Kate What did you do? Were you an only child?

Gemma Yeh. Phoned my mum's sister in London. Said she'd meet
me at Kings Cross off the train but she wasn't there, and when I
phoned again they said number unavailable and I haven't seen her
since.

Kate How can things go wrong like that?
Gemma All the time when you're me. I went to a hotel and that took
    all the money I had. In one night. After that it was the streets.
Kate For eight years?
Gemma I've been in hostels, lived in squats, had a room in a pub
    but had to work sixteen hours a day for nothing, moved in with a
    bloke but he died as well.

Kate looks at her

    He just got ill and died. And somebody stole our dog. I don't know
    why you want to write about all that.
Kate I don't. I want to write about what happens from now on.
Gemma I wanted to change everything so I hitched a lift and ended
    up here and nothing changed.
Kate Until yesterday.
Gemma Some well-meaning woman took me in for a night. It's
    happened before. It won't last.
Kate This time it's Dorcas.
Gemma So? (*She looks at Kate*)
Kate Dorcas means it.
Gemma We'll see.
Kate It's not the sort of thing she normally does.
Gemma That's why it won't last.
Kate That's what I want to write about.
Gemma I think she's a frustrated do-gooder looking for a new
    cause.
Kate She doesn't need a new cause. She's got Vincent.
Gemma He's an old cause.
Kate Aren't you grateful to her?
Gemma She should be grateful to me, shouldn't she? For being in
    need?

Pause

Kate Can I quote you? (*She makes notes*)

Black-out

SCENE 5

The same. Later that day

*Gemma is still in the dressing-gown. She has smoked nearly all the
cigarettes, using a plant pot as an ashtray. She seems to have done
nothing else*

*Dorcas and Vincent return from work with Sholto in tow. Vincent
carries a plastic bag*

Dorcas Gemma, hallo! We're back.
Vincent We're back.
Sholto We're back.
Dorcas Sholto usually waits in the car whilst I drop Vincent off then
    I drive him home whilst Vincent has a bath, but they both wanted
    to come and see you.
Gemma You make them sound like two-year-olds.
Dorcas Do I?
Gemma In fact that's probably why they act like two-year-olds.

Beat

Dorcas What have you been doing?
Gemma Nothing. (*To Vincent*) Do you want a cigarette?
Vincent Who?
Gemma You.

*Vincent looks at Dorcas who is still thinking about Gemma's
previous remark and says nothing*

Vincent I don't smoke.
Gemma Doesn't Dorcas like it?
Vincent I don't like it.
Gemma (*to Sholto*) Do you?
Sholto Umm ...
Vincent No.

Sholto No.
Gemma (*to Dorcas*) Do you?
Dorcas Wasted on me. You keep them for yourself.

Gemma lights a cigarette. Vincent and Sholto are obviously excited

Vincent (*holding up the plastic bag*) We found you a present.
Dorcas You were going to clean it before giving it to Gemma,
   Vincent.
Sholto On the tip.
Dorcas And yourself.
Gemma What is it?
Dorcas Gemma might not like it.

Vincent looks crestfallen

Gemma I might.

*Vincent gets out a large, nicely carved but mucky wooden dog and
holds it out to Gemma*

Vincent It's a dog!
Sholto 'Cos you've got a dog's name.

Gemma looks at it in silence

Dorcas I told them you might not like it.
Sholto Has it got a name, Vinny?
Gemma Chummy. He's called Chummy. (*She doesn't move to
   take it*)
Vincent You don't like it.
Sholto Oh dear.
Gemma He's just like my Chummy. Just the same. Those eyes ...

Silence

Dorcas Come on, Sholto, I'll take you home.

Sholto turns sadly to go. Gemma takes the dog and hugs it to her. This makes Sholto happy

Vincent I found it.
Gemma Did you? (*She strokes the dog*)

Vincent is happy

Dorcas relaxes and follows Sholto out

Vincent Shall I wash it for you?
Gemma My Chummy was a smelly dog.
Vincent Where is he?
Gemma Someone took him.
Vincent To wash?
Gemma Perhaps he's now a nice clean dog living in a nice clean house.
Vincent Yes.
Gemma How old are you?
Vincent Old enough to know better! (*He laughs*)
Gemma Than what?

He thinks

Vincent Than — break things. Talk with my mouth open.
Gemma You can't talk with it closed.
Vincent Eat. Forget my bag. Get dirty.
Gemma You're stupid, aren't you?
Vincent Yes.
Gemma So long as you know.
Vincent Everybody's stupid sometimes.
Gemma Not Dorcas.
Vincent Yes! She does stupid things sometimes.
Gemma Surely not?
Vincent One of them was she forgot to go in the garage for some petrol and we were going to the day centre and the car stopped before we got there.

Gemma I wish that had happened to me.
Vincent Do you?
Gemma I wouldn't have run over my mother.

Vincent laughs because he thinks it's a joke

Don't.

He has another burst of laughter

Stop it. It's not funny.

She slaps his face. He stops

Vincent I'm old enough to know better?
Gemma You don't laugh when someone's run over their mother.
Vincent In a car?
Gemma I knocked her over and she fell down and I drove over her.
Vincent Didn't you like her?
Gemma That's why you're stupid. She was my mother and I loved
    her and I ran her over.
Vincent I think *that's* stupid.
Gemma It was an accident!
Vincent A stupid accident.
Gemma What are you in this world for?
Vincent I don't know.
Gemma You don't do anything useful. What's the point of you?
Vincent I made a yo-yo.
Gemma Why didn't you make this dog, eh? Why can't you do
    something useful? Instead of finding it on a rubbish tip.
Vincent I rescued it.
Gemma It's a fucking stupid smelly old dog and whoever threw it
    out threw it out because it was rubbish. Like you.
Vincent Only on Wednesdays.
Gemma What?
Vincent On Wednesdays I'm rubbish. Tuesdays and Thursdays
    I'm day centre, Fridays I'm gardening, Mondays I'm gardening,
    Saturdays I'm shopping and Sundays I'm resting. Like you.

Gemma Like me?

Vincent You're resting today. You rest on Wednesdays. What do you do on Sundays?

Gemma Nothing.

Vincent Mondays?

Gemma Nothing.

Vincent Tuesdays, Wednesdays, and Fridays?

Gemma Nothing.

Vincent Saturdays!

Gemma Nothing!

Vincent What's the point of *you*?

Gemma starts to cry

Gemma Nothing, nothing, nothing ...

Vincent enthusiastically hugs her better

Vincent Don't cry.

She struggles and he hugs her tighter

Gemma Get off me. Get off. (*She kicks and butts him*)

Vincent Don't do that.

Gemma *Get off!*

Dorcas enters

They struggle apart

Kate follows Dorcas in

Dorcas Vincent, what's happening?

Gemma He attacked me.

Vincent She was crying.

Gemma I couldn't get him off me.

Dorcas What did you do to Gemma, Vincent?
Vincent I hugged her.
Dorcas What for?
Gemma What the hell do you think?
Vincent Make her feel better.
Gemma He's the same as all the rest of them.
Dorcas No, he isn't.
Gemma He doesn't do rape then?

Kate starts to make notes

Dorcas He hasn't touched you!
Gemma You saw him! You came in and saw him! (*She turns to Kate*) You saw him.
Kate He attacked you? For no reason?
Gemma (*to Dorcas*) You left him alone with me. Filthy old man.
Dorcas Vincent, go and wash and change.
Gemma *Filthy filthy.* I don't mean his overalls.
Vincent She was crying.
Kate Why was she crying, Vincent?
Gemma He was going to rape me.
Vincent Because there's no point to her.

Vincent goes out, taking the wooden dog with him

Dorcas I'm sure you misunderstood.
Gemma Are you? So we're not going to the police then?
Dorcas I don't think ——
Gemma He assaulted me!
Dorcas He didn't mean any harm.
Gemma Like the others? You insisted I went to the police about them.

Beat

Changed your mind? Think I made it up? (*She turns to Kate*) Writing this all down? Dorcas doesn't believe me now.

Dorcas Vincent has never harmed anyone in his life.

Gemma Me! Look at the state I'm in. I'm traumatized. Write that down.

Dorcas Don't write anything down.

Kate I'm a reporter.

Dorcas You're a friend.

Gemma She's a reporter! It was your idea!

Dorcas I've only been gone fifteen minutes. Vincent was perfectly all right when I left. He wouldn't attack you.

Gemma You don't know what he does when you're not there.

Dorcas I do. I do. Brian at the Day Centre tells me. Phil at the tip and Jeff at the nursery where he works ....

Gemma Now I'm telling you.

Dorcas I think it's the state you're in.

Gemma He'll love you to death, you said.

Dorcas He's gentle. Honestly, he's gentle, isn't he, Kate?

Kate Boisterous, maybe.

Dorcas You've just misunderstood.

Gemma You don't believe me.

Dorcas Maybe it was something you said.

Gemma My fault?

Dorcas He's not used to having guests. It's a new experience for him.

Gemma Your fault then. (*She lights a cigarette*)

Dorcas Yes. It probably is. I didn't think it through ...

Gemma Do-gooders never do.

Dorcas I'd rather you didn't smoke.

Gemma Do you?

Dorcas It's bad for everybody's health.

Gemma I can't manage without.

Dorcas Perhaps you could smoke outside then.

Gemma Perhaps you want to throw me out.

Silence

(*To Kate*) I told you.

Dorcas No, I'm just trying to understand.

Gemma What are you going to do about him?
Dorcas I don't know.
Gemma Nothing. Hope I'll go away and forget all about it? Rape
  is a terrible thing, you said. You have to do something about it.
Dorcas Vincent didn't rape you.
Gemma He was going to!
Dorcas No he wasn't! This is ridiculous.

Kate is writing

Stop it. Stop writing. I'm not giving my permission for you to
write about this.
Gemma I am.
Dorcas No! If this nonsense gets in the paper, the police *will* be
  round asking Vincent all sorts of questions and he won't be able
  to make any sense of his answers and they won't believe him. No-
  one will believe him and they'll think the worse.
Gemma And now you know how I feel. There's no-one in the
  whole world who'll stand up for me.

Vincent, singing "Hey Jude", enters with a nice clean wooden dog

Vincent He's now a nice clean dog living in a nice clean house. (*He
  puts Chummy down on the floor*) Here, Chummy, Chummy,
  Chummy. I've had an idea.

Silence

Kate What's that?
Vincent It's a thing in your head.
Kate Oh.

Beat

Get it out then.
Vincent You can write it down.

Kate nods. Silence

Kate What is it?
Vincent When we were making the yo-yos, Brian said, "I could do
with some help."

Silence

Kate Making the yo-yos?
Vincent And everything. Brian said, "Do any of you know anyone
who could come to the centre and help me?" And I know Gemma.
(*He turns to Gemma*) Brian needs help. And you are very skilful
with yo-yos. (*He holds out the yo-yo*)

Silence

I bet Sholto doesn't know anyone.

Gemma takes the yo-yo

Gemma I'm very tired.
Dorcas Go to bed then. Have you eaten anything?

Gemma shakes her head. She doesn't want anything to eat

Gemma There's no lock on the door.
Vincent Chummy could keep invaders out.

Gemma says nothing, picks up Chummy and starts to go

Vincent Can you come tomorrow?

Gemma hesitates a moment

There would be a point to you then.

Gemma goes out

Vincent turns his music on then turns it off quickly as he remembers that Gemma can't sleep with it on

Dorcas Put it on if you want, Vincent. We can't spend all evening being quiet.

Vincent turns the music on

Kate Trying to drive her out?
Dorcas Just not quite so loud, eh?

Vincent turns the music down

(*Picking up Kate's pad*) What happens in the end?
Kate I'm not making it up.
Dorcas Do you have a sex life, Kate?
Kate What …?
Dorcas I don't.
Kate No.
Dorcas What you've never had, you don't miss. Do you think that's true?
Kate Well, is it?
Dorcas By and large.

They look at Vincent

Do you think it's the same for Vincent?

Beat

Kate You want me to ask him?

Dorcas doesn't reply. She exits to the kitchen

Vincent, what do you think of Gemma?
Vincent The dog?
Kate No, Gemma, the young woman.

Vincent She's a bit mixed up.
Kate Have you ever thought of getting married?
Vincent To Gemma?
Kate To anyone.
Vincent I couldn't leave Dorcas.
Kate Or having a family? Or having sex?

Vincent looks at her

Vincent No, no.
Kate No.
Vincent A lot of things are for other people. A few things are for
    me.
Kate A few things?
Vincent I'm not clever enough for a lot of things. I would be
    unhappy.

Kate nods

Kate You're wise. Just to have a few things.

Black-out

SCENE 6

The same. The next morning

*Vincent and Dorcas are having breakfast. He is singing "With a
Little Help From My Friends" in between rounds of toast*

*Gemma enters as he gets to the chorus and joins in quietly. She is
dressed and has a outdoor jacket over her arm*

Dorcas Do you want some breakfast?
Gemma Yes please.

Vincent pours her out some cereals which overflow the plate

Vincent Oh.
Gemma It's all right. I'm very hungry. (*She scoops them up*)
Dorcas Are you going out?
Vincent Yes.
Dorcas I know *you* are.
Vincent To the day centre.
Dorcas I know!
Gemma Me too.
Vincent You can sit in the back with Sholto.
Dorcas To the day centre?
Vincent Yes.
Gemma Vincent said …
Dorcas Yes, but …
Vincent Brian needs help.
Gemma Bad idea?
Vincent Brilliant idea.
Dorcas Yes. OK. You'll get on. Brian smokes.
Gemma OK.
Vincent OK.

They eat

Curtain

FURNITURE AND PROPERTY LIST

Scene 1

On stage: 3 easy chairs
Dining-table
4 chairs
Cassette player with tapes
Telephone
Cupboard. *In it*: 4 glasses
Pot plant

Off stage: Plastic bags containing old clothes (**Dorcas**)
Pile of *Big Issue* copies (**Gemma**)
Bag (**Vincent**)

Personal: **Vincent**: yellow yo-yo

Scene 2

Strike: **Vincent**'s bag

Set: Mug of tea for **Vincent**

Off stage: Empty mug (**Gemma**)

Scene 3

Set: Tray, used plates, cutlery, etc. on the dining-table

Off stage: Bag containing notebook, pen, copy of local newspaper (**Kate**)

2 halves of broken plastic plate (**Vincent**)
Carrier bag containing large plastic bottle of beer (**Sholto**)

Personal: **Kate**: wrist-watch
                Sholto: red yo-yo

SCENE 4

Strike: Tray and contents from dining-table
                Kate's bag, notebook, pen, local newspaper
                4 glasses of beer, bottle of beer
                Red and yellow yo-yos

Off stage: Mug of coffee (**Gemma**)
                Bag containing notebook, pen (**Kate**)
                Mug of coffee (**Kate**)
                Box of matches (**Gemma**)

Personal: **Kate**: packet of cigarettes in jacket pocket

SCENE 5

Strike: **Kate**'s bag, notebook and pen, almost full packet of cigarettes

Set: Almost empty cigarette packet
                Cigarette stubs in pot plant

Off stage: Plastic carrier containing large carved, mucky wooden dog
                    (**Vincent**)
                Bag containing notebook, pen (**Kate**)
                Clean carved wooden dog (**Vincent**)

SCENE 6

Set: Plates, bowls, mugs, cutlery, toast, packet of cereal, milk

Off stage: Outdoor jacket (**Gemma**)

LIGHTING PLOT

Property fittings required: nil

Interior. The same scene throughout

To open: Full general lighting

Cue 1   **Vincent** sings   (Page 11)
   Black-out. When ready bring up lighting for Scene 2

Cue 2   **Gemma**: "It's easy." Pause   (Page 13)
   Black-out. When ready bring up lighting for Scene 3

Cue 3   **Gemma** turns and goes out up to bed   (Page 22)
   Black-out. When ready bring up bright sunshine
      effect for Scene 4

Cue 4   **Kate** makes notes   (Page 25)
   Black-out. When ready bring up lighting for Scene 5

Cue 5   **Kate**: "Just to have a few things."   (Page 36)
   Black-out. When ready bring up lighting for Scene 6

EFFECTS PLOT

Please read the notice on page v concerning the use of copyright music

Cue 1	**Dorcas** goes out to the kitchen *Phone rings*	(Page 10)
Cue 2	To open SCENE 2 *Tape of Beatles' music plays*	(Page 11)
Cue 3	**Dorcas** turns the music down *Reduce volume*	(Page 11)
Cue 4	To open SCENE 3 *Beatles' music playing from kitchen*	(Page 13)
Cue 5	**Vincent**: "No. It's my job." *Doorbell*	(Page 14)
Cue 6	**Kate**: " … with her bachelor brother …" *Increase music volume from kitchen*	(Page 14)
Cue 7	**Dorcas**: "Turn it down!" *Reduce music volume from kitchen*	(Page 15)
Cue 8	**Dorcas**: "I don't know!" *Crashing from kitchen*	(Page 16)
Cue 9	**Kate**: "It's your story." *Doorbell*	(Page 17)
Cue 10	**Vincent** switches on music in sitting-room *Another Beatles' tape plays in sitting-room*	(Page 19)

www.ingramcontent.com/pod-product-compliance
Ingram Content Group UK Ltd.
Pitfield, Milton Keynes, MK11 3LW, UK
UKHW021822150726
7214IPUK00017B/269